D0596015

STRESSED

OUT

STUDENTS

GUIDE

TO

DEALING

WITH

TESTS

STRESSED OUT STUDENTS GUIDE TO DEALING WITH TESTS

Series Editor
Lisa Medoff, Ph.D.

KAPLAN

© 2008 Kaplan, Inc.

Published by Kaplan Publishing, a division of Kaplan, Inc.
1 Liberty Plaza, 24th Floor
New York, NY 10006

Printed in the United States of America

First printing: 2008
10 9 8 7 6 5 4 3 2 1

SOS: Stressed Out Students' Guide to Dealing with Tests
ISBN-13: 978-1-4277-9808-4

Kaplan Publishing books are available at special quantity discounts to use for sales promotions, employee premiums, or educational purposes. Please email our Special Sales Department to order or for more information at kaplanpublishing@kaplan.com, or write to Kaplan Publishing, 1 Liberty Plaza, 24th Floor, New York, NY 10006.

Got stress?

Learn how to handle the pressures and
demands of test-taking in today's ultra
competitive environment.

Stories and real-life advice told *by*
teens *for* teens to help cope with
stress—for students and parents alike.

ABOUT THE SERIES EDITOR

Lisa Medoff holds a B.A in psychology from Rice University, an M.S.Ed. in school counseling from the University of Pennsylvania, and a Ph.D. in child and adolescent development from Stanford University.

For the past ten years, Lisa has been working with middle and high school students who have learning disabilities and emotional disorders. In this job, Lisa consults with both families and schools to help them provide the optimal school and home environments for their children with special needs.

She has taught child & adolescent development and psychology courses to both undergraduates and teacher credential candidates at Stanford University, Santa Clara University and San Jose State University.

Lisa works with the non-profit Cleo Eulau Center of Palo Alto, providing consulting services and teacher education workshops for elementary school teachers in a high-risk school district. She is also the author of a weekly child psychology column for the website Education.com.

CONTENTS

CONTENTS

CONTENTS

CONTENTS

CONTENTS

CONTENTS

INTRODUCTION

My poor college students. They have to hear the same speech every time I pass back a test. That's what they get for taking a class with a psychology professor who also works with kids that have school difficulties. The speech usually goes something like this:

"This test is not a judgment of your worth as a person. This test is only a reflection of how well you know the information that was covered in the last few chapters. It is a measurement of your performance at one point in time. A test is a way for you to figure out what you already know, and what you still need to learn. That is all a test is really for."

"Your grade is not an indication of much I like you. Nor is it an indication of how smart you are, if you are good enough to make it at this school, or if you should or should not be a psychology major. It is not a prediction of how successful you will be in life."

"If you did not get the grade that you wanted, it means one thing, and one thing only: you need to put in more time studying for the next test. If

INTRODUCTION

you feel that you did put in a lot of time studying, then perhaps you need to change your strategy. Look over every question that you missed, and understand why you got it wrong. The reasons that we give for the events in our lives influence our behavior in the future. You can sit back and blame me for giving a test that is unfair or too hard, but that probably won't cause you to work any harder next time, and it won't improve your grade."

"If you are happy with your grade, then take care not to get lazy. Put in the same amount of effort to study for the next test. For those of you that would like to improve your grade, please come see me during office hours. I would be happy to talk about how you can prepare for the next exam."

I hate passing back tests. I think I get more anxious than the students do. That's why I give that little (okay, long) speech. To protect myself from the glares I get from the students who didn't do so well. If you came into my class right after I passed back tests, you would be able to tell from the looks on the students' faces who did well and who didn't. Those who did well are staring at me with delighted adoration — I'm the

INTRODUCTION

best, most brilliant professor in the whole world, and they're ready to take down every word I say. The ones who didn't do so well are calling me all kinds of names in their heads (most of them probably unfit to print here without the use of symbols) and starting to tune me out. Those are the students I give the speech for – I'm trying to win them back and convince them to keep trying.

My tests are hard. I think they're pretty fair – I don't test about obscure names or dates, or about minor studies that I didn't mention in class. But they're hard. I try to ask difficult questions that involve a bit of thinking. Questions that you couldn't answer with common sense or by knowing a few basic test-taking tips. When tests are hard, you have to really earn your grade. You have to really know the information. The information that still sticks with me to this day comes from classes where the professors gave really hard tests. I may not have liked the teacher at the time, but I sure did learn. That's what school is for – to learn information. Students pay a lot of money in tuition, and I wouldn't be giving them their money's worth by simply handing out A's to everyone.

INTRODUCTION

I think most college professors feel this way. We love our subjects. We're passionate about what we're teaching you, and we want you to be, too. But we're also a little defensive about the academic club we belong to. We don't want to admit just anyone — we have to have our standards, or else our profession will start to lose respect. We have an obligation to the rest of the people in our field (and an obligation to our clients, patients, or readers) to uphold the standards of our profession. When I give someone a good grade, I'm saying to the people who are going to let that person into their graduate school or give that student a job, "Yeah, she knows her stuff." That's a big responsibility, and I don't take it lightly.

Your teachers in high school are coming from the same place. They have an obligation to tell the colleges that you are applying to, "Yeah, this student knows his stuff. He's a hard worker, and he knows how to study, so he's ready for the next level of challenge."

Tests are for teachers as well. We use them to see how well we are teaching. If you fail a test, then I have to take some responsibility for

INTRODUCTION

that. Wait, you're not totally off the hook. You must put in the time to study on your own. But the test is useful for us as teachers to see if we need to change the way we are presenting the information. So tests are not just instruments of evil to ruin your weekend by forcing you to study on Saturday night. They're helpful tools for both teachers and students. There, don't you love tests now?

Does this mean that I think tests are wonderful and perfect? Of course not. I think there are a lot of really smart people out there that are just not good test-takers. There are also a lot of people who are really good at their jobs that got horrible grades in school. Tests are only one way for teachers to figure out if you know the information. They're usually the easiest, fastest, and most practical way to understand what a large group of people knows. But they're not the only way. I wish that I could spend hours talking with every one of my students so that I could understand exactly what they know and what kind of thinkers they are, but it's just not possible.

INTRODUCTION

So if you're not great at taking tests, make some effort to improve your study skills, but don't be too hard on yourself. This book can help you on both fronts. We'll tell you more about why tests are necessary and why it's important to learn how to take them well. You'll find some great study tips and ideas that will come in handy when you're actually taking tests. We've even included a chapter about pacing yourself that you can show your parents when they're asking you why you're taking a break when you have a big math test tomorrow. You'll get some info about big standardized tests like the SATs and the APs. We'll even help you work through the scary idea of failing and tell you how to reward yourself when you do well.

You may not love taking tests. But would you really want to do away with them completely? Do you want an operation from a doctor whose professors just had a feeling he knew the information? If you were accused of a crime, would you want a lawyer who just really, really loved the law, but couldn't pass her bar exam? Here's an auto mechanic who cheated on his certification test — want him to check your brakes for you?

INTRODUCTION

The earlier you start getting into good study habits, the easier the transition to college will be. College tests are harder than high school tests. They cover more material, and the professor will give you less guidance about what exactly will be on the test. I have found that the students who come into college with good study skills have the easiest time adjusting to the entire college experience – they don't get overwhelmed and they enjoy their time so much more right from the start.

Since tests are a necessary part of your life, start reading this book and find out information about how to improve your performance on them unless you're looking at this book because you're putting off studying for that science test. In that case, go study a little, and read this later!

Lisa Medoff, Ph.D.

CHAPTER 4

HOW TO USE THIS BOOK

Chill (Relax)

Absorb more information and practical advice.

FOOD FOR THOUGHT

A study conducted by the University of Michigan found that 1/3 of teens feel stressed out on a daily basis. The leading cause? The feeling of not being able to meet high expectations. Prolonged feelings of stress can lead to frustration, illness, aggression, and depression.

Read these inspirational, witty, or tongue-in-cheek observations that you can use to motivate yourself—or just for fun.

F reaking out. Flipping out. Spazzing. Call it what you want, but one thing's for sure: it's not a good thing to do during a test, although it certainly is easy to do!

Maybe you studied more than you've ever studied before and are psyching yourself out that it'll all be for nothing. Maybe you're encountering tougher questions than you expected. Maybe you're wondering if you maybe studied the wrong chapter!

In any case, it won't do you any good to go ballistic. When you're stressing out, you're not thinking clearly and you're more likely to second

A problem is a chance for you to do your best.
—Duke Ellington

HOW TO USE THIS BOOK

We created the SOS series to help you find answers to questions most pressing on your mind. In developing this series, we brought together both adult and teen experts who shared their successes and struggles. Here's how to best use this book:

guess your answers and waste more time mulling them over than if you're confident and calm. So if you find yourself sweating under the collar, take a second to breathe deeply, focus, and chill out. It's the best thing you can do for yourself during a test.

F.Y.I.

A few simple ways to manage stress:

1. Positive "Self-Talk" : Try repeating to yourself silently "I can handle this" or "It's going to be O.K." Having a positive attitude can make stress dissapear.

2. See the funny side of life! Look at your situation from a comical perspective and you'll be able to relax, and when you're relaxed you can think more clearly.

DR. LISA SAYS...

When you get the test, take a minute to empty out everything that is cluttering up your brain before you look at any of the questions. Write down all of your mnemonics, formulas, or information that you're afraid that you'll forget or get confused about. This will not only serve as practical help, but it will also calm you down by focusing you on the information, not on the difficulty of the test. You'll see how much you really do know, and you'll be able to tackle the questions with confidence.

> Get expert advice and anecdotes from our series editor, Lisa Medoff, Ph.D.

> Absorb more information and practical advice.

HOW TO USE THIS BOOK

Think kids are the only ones who need to learn something? Advice, inside info, and motivation for the know-it-alls in every kid's life.

Look here for basic info and terminology

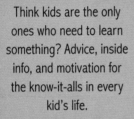

118 FIGHTING OFF WHAT'S FIGHTING YOU: STRESS

CHAPTER 12

Fighting Off Wh

What Is It and How Can

I'm so stressed," is heard your friends Recently, you even fi them when they con of homework they h commitments. But w

PARENT SPEAK

Let's face it, adults know stress. But do you understand how much stress your student is under? A recent poll of high school students revealed that a whopping 70% said that they feel stressed "most of the time." What stress management tools can you share with your kid? Are there experiences you can relate that will help them put things in perspective?

THE BASICS

stress

n. a specific respon lus, as fear or pain, with the normal phy organism.

physical, mental, or "Worry over his job under a great stres

a situation, occurre "The stress of beir gave him a poundi

HOW TO USE THIS BOOK

CHAPTER 12

Fighting You: Stress Management

id of It?

ou've probably
t a daily basis.
niming in with
he mounds
r after school
eally??

Stress is the way your body reacts to demands placed on it, whether that's your upcoming advanced Algebra exam or dealing with a difficult friend. When you feel stressed by something, your body releases chemicals into your bloodstream. These chemicals can have both positive and negative effects. Sometimes stress makes you work harder to get something done, but stress can also slow you down, especially if you have no way to deal with the extra energy the chemicals produce in you.

o a stimu-
interferes
rium of an

Here, we'll help you understand the causes of stress, signs of stress, how stress affects you, and the best ways to deal with it, because when you've already got so much to do, stress is the last thing you need to worry about.

or tension:
ealth put him

using this:
elevator

> For fast-acting relief, try slowing down. **99**
>
> —Lily Tomlin

FOOD FOR THOUGHT

Many studies suggest that as students get to college, their sleeping schedule suffers greatly. Lack of sleep often results in the inability to concentrate, the need for more naps, and constant fatigue. Try getting a good rest and maybe this will give you more strength to deal with school and other issues.

STRESSED OUT
STUDENTS
GUIDE TO
DEALING WITH
TESTS

The Dreaded Tests—What The

> My philosophy is that not only are you responsible for your life, but doing the best at this moment puts you in the best place for the next moment.
> —Oprah Winfrey

When you're a teen, you may think that the foulest four-letter word in the English language is spelled T-E-S-T.

Unfortunately for you, when it comes to your opinion of tests and most adults' opinions on them, you're batting for different teams. You'll always feel that you could do with a lot fewer, while your parents, your teachers, the school district, and the state and the universities can't seem to dole out enough. Since it's the adults that call the shots, what you get is an endless string of subject tests in your classes, at every grade level, and as you near your college years, a barrage of state-issued standardized tests.

THE BASICS

test
n. the means by which the presence, quality, or genuineness of anything is determined; a means of trial.

Definition from dictionary.com

Are, Why They're Necessary

Newsflash: It doesn't end there! Once you're in college, there will be midterms and finals for every class, quarter and semester, and once you graduate, there will be graduate school tests (the GREs, the LSATs, the GMAT's, the MCAT'S, etc.).

So what does this all mean? Unfortunately, it means that whining won't do a thing for your future. Tests are built into our society and education systems as benchmarks for success. It's time to beef up your test-taking skills so that while others complain, you're sailing past the competition.

DR. LISA SAYS...

Learn how to study NOW. Most failures that I see at the college level are because students do not know how to study properly. Sometimes being smart can work against you because you can slide by without doing much work. Paying attention in class may be enough to get by in high school, so you never have to crack a book. Eventually that changes — you get to a point where you just can't compete without putting in the effort. Many college professors use textbooks only to supplement their lectures, so you can't get by without going to class AND doing the reading.

The What (What They're Testing For)

FOOD FOR THOUGHT

According to the National Center for Education, total undergraduate enrollment is on the rise and expected to reach new heights with each year. In fact, 15 million students are currently pursuing their undergraduate degree, and by the year 2017 this number is projected to reach 17 million!

You hear it from the news: there are more and more college applicants every year. You hear it from your parents: you need to get good grades to be competitive when it's time to apply. You hear it from your teachers and school counselors: you need to have a stellar transcript and a laundry list of extracurricular activities if you want to get into the college of your choice.

Ever watched a fast food employee working hard for long hours and low pay? Know someone who is that worker? Dream jobs usually require education and hard work. Chances are you have some high aspirations for your future self, and therein lies the first clue into understanding why tests are a necessary evil.

Everyone wants a piece of the pie; it's as simple as that. And in a society where everyone is competing for success, there have to be measures of who deserves success over others. It's an imperfect system, but tests are the hurdles you'll have to leap to prove you're better, smarter, and more willing to work at studying than your peers.

Tests test you. They test your ability to perform, and they push you to keep on jumping hurdles, to keep moving forward towards achieving your professional and personal goals.

> "The best way out is always through."
> —Robert Frost

TIME CRUNCH

How would you manage your time in the following situation?

There's a school dance tonight and your crush has asked you to go to it. The dance runs from 6 PM to 9 PM, and it's now 3 PM. Oh yeah, and there's a five-chapter history test tomorrow you haven't studied for. How much time would you spend…

Shopping for something to wear?_____

At the dance? _____

Studying? _____

Eating? _____

Sleeping? _____

The Why (Why You Need to Do Well)

Obviously, some tests are going to be more important in shaping your path than others. Screwing up on one test in a history class is not going to doom you to a career in fast-food services, or keep you out of all the respectable colleges in the nation. Not being able to perform at a certain level on a test like the SATs however, might have a slightly more significant impact.

Suffice it to say, it's best to develop your studying and testing skills early so that you'll be able to do just as well as you like on all tests, great and

FOOD FOR THOUGHT

A 2008 survey by a national consumer research group found that over 70% of teens rate themselves as happy with their friends, talents, grades, health, and family members.

The beautiful thing about learning is nobody can take it away from you.

—B.B. King

small. The study skills you develop through taking a really difficult math class at school will be there for you when you face off against the math section of the SATs. Studying for an Advanced Placement (AP) test in English Composition is going to help you on the verbal and analytical writing section of the SATs and the final exams in your English college courses.

Basically, there's no downside to developing good study and test-taking skills NOW.

THE BASICS

cheat

v. To act dishonestly; practice fraud. To violate rules deliberately. To deceive by trickery. To mislead; fool.

Definition from dictionary.com

"All of the top achievers I know are life-long learners... looking for new skills, insights, and ideas. If they're not learning, they're not growing... not moving towards excellence."

—David Waitely

The How (How You'll Ace Them)

DR. LISA SAYS...

Feeling stressed about school? Talk to your teachers. Tell them exactly what is stressing you out and ask for help sorting out your workload. I am almost always willing to make accommodations for students (extensions, alternative assignments, extra practice questions), as long as they ask me ahead of time. Not all teachers are willing to help, but it can't hurt to ask. Don't be afraid to ask for what you want — the worst someone can do is say no.

Let's cut to the chase: you're only going to ace tests by developing the set of study skills, habits, and methods that work for you. Some people study best in their own rooms, while others have to be in a public place like a library or café with a lot of background noise. Some people take notes on index cards, some highlight right in their books. Some methods work best for some subjects, while others work better for others.

"Self-trust is the first secret of success."

——Ralph Waldo Emerson

Basically, it's a bit like alchemy. You're mixing and developing your personal formulas for success, and tests are the gauges you use to determine the effectiveness of the methods you've been trying.

A pinch of creativity, a dash of ingenuity, and a load of hard work will turn you into a test-taking whiz. Let's begin.

F.Y.I.

How are your note-taking skills?

Do you tend to copy down exactly what is in the book? Have you developed a system of abbreviations and symbols that allow you to shrink loads of information into just a few sentences? If not, practice making outlines of chapters in your textbook and improving these skills.

"Where much is expected from an individual, he may rise to the level of events and make the dream come true."

—Elbert Hubbard

Get With It – Developing

> The difference between school and life? In school, you're taught a lesson and then given a test. In life, you're given a test that teaches you a lesson.
>
> —Tom Bodett

With things like subject tests and standardized tests, a common complaint of teens and parents is that sometimes exams don't really test how intelligent you are, but really just seem to test for how well you take tests.

This is both good news and bad news. First, the bad: if you're a genius in certain areas—say, outdoor survival methods or inventing practical machines—they may serve you in your future job one day, but until that day comes, those smarts won't likely be reflected in test scores or your grades.

F.Y.I.

Study Skills Tip

Understanding is more important than memorizing. Making sure you understand a subject also helps you to retain it in memory longer, and makes it easier to study subjects built on the same concepts.

Good Study Skills

The good news: if there is indeed a way to ace the skill of test-taking, you can do well in even those subjects where you don't have natural smarts. If you're not a math genius, for example, you can still get far by writing the formulas down on cards and reviewing them over and over so you can plug in the right numbers on test day. If your English skills are not the best, you can still beef up your writing by memorizing loads and loads of impressive vocabulary words to drop into your sentences.

All of this is to say that if you spend some time honing your test-taking skills, you can benefit big time. So get with it, and you'll get some pretty nice returns.

FOOD FOR THOUGHT

According to a Penn State University Publication, "Everything that we encounter through our senses passes through our sensory memory. In order for learning to take place, three important processes must occur in the brain: attention & pattern recognition, working memory storage, and encoding." Therefore, sharpening memorization skills when studying could help us retain large chunks of information for longer periods of time.

"The journey of a thousand miles begins with a step."

—Lao-tzu

In the Zone (Getting in the Right Frame

FOOD FOR THOUGHT

Is the TV a constant distraction in your house that may be sucking up your study time?

Fact: 52% of kids ages 5-17 have TVs in their bedrooms.

Fact: On average, a typical US home has the TV on 7 hours and 12 minutes a day.

It's time to stop seeing tests as those annoying things that you just have to do and get out of the way. Not taking a test seriously can mean missing out on a good opportunity to challenge yourself and to grow into an individual who's primed for success in our society.

When it's test time, it's game time. You wouldn't go into a championship game without practicing the week before, would you (who are you, Allen Iverson?). When you're being tested, you're being invited to show what you can do. You're being told to bring it.

"Opportunity is missed by most people because it is dressed in overalls and looks like work."

—Thomas Edison

ind)

Mark tests down on a calendar so you can see them coming a mile away. Get it into your head that the results of the test are important, and convince yourself that you have to do well on it, and that you can do well on it. You will.

DR. LISA SAYS...

If you have trouble with procrastination, try doing something small and mindless just to get you started, since making yourself sit down and get to work is usually the hardest part. Write out flashcards, organize handouts, or put sticky notes on the pages with the important formulas. Just think one step at a time. Once you've started working, you'll usually slip into the harder stuff without thinking about it too much. If you still have trouble with procrastination, rely on a timer. Tell yourself you only have to work for 15 minutes – you can handle 15 little minutes, can't you? Set the timer, study for 15 minutes, and then set the timer for a short break. Then tackle another 15 minutes.

"No man ever reached to excellence in any one art or profession without having passed through the slow and painful process of study and preparation."

—Horace
(ancient Roman poet)

Base of Operations (Your Study Space)

FOOD FOR THOUGHT
Study Skills Tip

When picking a place to study, avoid your bed. It's just way too tempting to put your head down and doze off.

" Do it now. You become successful the moment you start moving toward a worthwhile goal. "
—Uknown

So you've established that your goal is to ace that upcoming test. You've located your target; you know your objective. It's time to set up your base of operations – your study space.

Your study space can be in your own home, or at a place where you know you can concentrate. It's important to locate the place or places where you'll spend most of your time studying because after a while, you'll start associating that place with work, and can get in the right frame of mind just by setting foot in it and opening up the books. When choosing a study space, consider:

✎ Noise: For some people, complete silence is necessary, but for others, a little bit of background noise helps. Decide which works for you and roll with it.

✎ Lighting: Brightly lit. Romantic "mood" lighting is great for a date, but not for a study session.

✎ Distractions: The space should be far away from distractions. That means loud conversations and other temptations that threaten to break your concentration.

✎ Convenience: If you have to spend half an hour getting there and getting set up there, you're just going to waste precious time. Look for a closer alternative.

✎ Proximity to food: Your brain is a highly metabolic organ, and when it is operating in high gear, you're going to get hungry. Fuel it with healthy snacks, kept close at hand.

DR. LISA SAYS...

Many freshmen fail their first college exams because they are not used to working at the intensity that is required at that level. They also find it quite easy to fall behind, since most college courses do not require daily work, or even class attendance, like high school classes do. That can leave a lot of time for playing video games and websurfing. However, the students that seem to do the best in my classes are the ones that tell me that they got used to working really hard in high school. For some of them, college even seems like less work and a lot more fun!

Let's Roll! (Setting Up a Study Schedule)

DR. LISA SAYS...

Being a good friend can also pay off for you, as well. The best way to make sure that you really know information is if you are able to teach it to someone else. Offer to help a friend study for a test, and make a specific time to get started. This appointment will lessen the chances of procrastination. Talking over the information will help you process it at a deeper level, which will help you remember it much better. It will also increase the chances that the information will actually stick with you after you've dumped it out of your brain and onto the test.

Setting up a study schedule is key if you're going to stay on track and be as prepared as you need to be before a test. The key here is to pace yourself. You're only going to exhaust yourself if you schedule in too much studying for one day, and you'll only be fooling yourself if you space it all out so much that you forget what you studied at the beginning of the schedule when you reach the end of it.

Once you've figured out what the best pace is for you, setting up your schedule is just a matter of writing down how many pages you want to study, your study objectives for the end of each session, and at what time you want to be done studying on each of those days. Schedule in some breaks so your brain can refresh itself before you get back into it full force.

The key is to stick to it. If you stick to your schedule, you won't find yourself in that horrible situation of having too many pages to read or memorize, and something like 30 minutes before the start of the test.

Aahhhhhhh!

TIME CRUNCH

How would you manage your time in the following situation?

You're the star player on your basketball team, and the championship game is coming up in a week. Your coach wants you and the rest of the team to spend 3 hours after school practicing. That means each day for the next five days, you'll be getting home at 6 PM. It just so happens that next week you also have 2 major tests. So this week, how much time each day do you spend…

Eating? _____

Studying? _____

Doing regular homework? _____

Relaxing? _____

Sleeping? _____

> The key is not to prioritize what's on your schedule, but to schedule your priorities.
>
> —Stephen R. Covey

Weapons of Mass Instruction (Tools Fo

FOOD FOR THOUGHT

Did you know that procrastination is one of the major contributors to high levels of stress among students? Don't procrastinate in preparing yourself with proper pencils, erasers, lead, Scantron answer sheets, and whiteout prior to a test. The test is stressful enough, be prepared with your supplies!

You've got your study space, your study schedule, and you're geared up and ready to roll. Things go a lot more smoothly and pleasantly if you have the right tools. "Pen, pencil and paper… what's there to think about?" you might be asking. A lot.

Writing utensils: Do you ever stop in the middle of writing so you can put your pen down and shake out your fingers? Have you ever put a pencil down to notice a nice red dent on your finger where it was pressing into your skin? Comfortable writing utensils are a must; it's not enough that they produce ink or lead marks. If you're having to push down unnecessarily hard or hav-

"There is nothing so likely to produce peace as to be well prepared to meet the enemy."

—George Washington

tudying)

ing to hold your hand in an awkward position for long periods of time, you're going to get tired of studying sooner. That's a no-brainer. Pick comfortable writing tools that write smoothly. And that squeaky highlighter that's running out of ink? That's not doing you any favors either.

Paper: Strain on your eyes will make you sleepy faster than anything you might do. If college-ruled paper or index cards with very tightly-spaced lines are causing you to squint, you're practically begging for sleepiness to overtake you sooner than it should.

" By failing to prepare you are preparing to fail. "
—Ben Franklin

DR. LISA SAYS...

Always ask for clarification or further explanation if you don't understand something in class. If you don't get a concept, tell the teacher. It's not a sign of stupidity to say that you don't understand something – asking questions tells the teacher that you are paying attention. You don't even have to do it in front of the class, although I guarantee that if you have a question, at least five other people who are also afraid to raise their hands have the same question, and they'll be grateful to you for asking.

Got Your Back (Study Groups)

S ometimes it becomes necessary to call in backup. Even Batman had Robin, and Superman occasionally needs the help of the entire Justice League.

If you're tackling a particularly difficult subject in preparation for an upcoming test study groups can provide the support you need. When it comes to advanced physics, calculus, or even literary analysis, sometimes two, three, or four heads are better than one.

FOOD FOR THOUGHT

Studies find that studying for large blocks of time is most beneficial in the memorization and learning process. So study for one hour straight and then take a 15-minute break to keep you going!

" I have never in my life learned anything from any man who agreed with me. "

—Dudley Field Malone

If you have to organize a group to make it happen, go ahead and take the reins. The key to leading successful study groups is not letting them turn into social gatherings. Set up a list or outline of topics or problems to be discussed and solved together so everyone stays on the same wavelength and can track the progress of the meeting as you give each other the boosts you need.

> A man only learns in two ways, one by reading, and the other by association with smarter people.
>
> —Will Rogers

F.Y.I.
Study Skills Tip

When putting together a study group, only invite people who are serious about studying. People who see gatherings as social events are only going to distract the ones who are there to learn.

Just Do It (Avoiding Procrastination)

W hen your TV and your video games or that cute guy or girl is staring you right in the face, it's can be more than a little difficult to see why it's so important to study now.

"I'll do it later," you'll say. But later comes along and then there's an invitation to go to the movies, or the newest episode of your favorite show on TV, and "later" turns into another "later" and so on and so forth until there just aren't any "laters" left and "now or never" is what's staring you in the face.

PARENT SPEAK

Parents can help their children get their work done by setting limits on activities that can be done prior to finishing homework or fulfilling a quota of study time. If grades and college do not motivate, then hopefully not being able to go to the mall before studying will!

"Procrastination is the grave in which opportunity is buried."

—Unknown

In short: don't procrastinate. Hopefully a study schedule will help avoid this, but you'll also be fighting that side of you that thinks of a million other things to do whenever you must do something for your own good.

"Just do it" isn't just helpful advice for star athletes. It's a pretty good message for teens that need to study, too.

THE BASICS

procrastinate

v. 1. To defer action; delay: to procrastinate until an opportunity is lost. 2. To put off till another day or time; defer; delay

Definition from dictionary.com

"The greatest amount of wasted time is the time not getting started."

—Dawson Trotman

Easy Does It—Study Trick

> "There are no secrets to success. It is the result of preparation, hard work, and learning from failure."
>
> —Colin Powell

Developing great test-taking skills can take years of practice and hard work and persistence.

But you want success NOW!

Of course you do. Until that day comes when you've nailed down the perfect study methods that work for you and the set of skills that will maximize your success on any test you take, there are a number of great shortcuts, tricks and devices that will improve your ability to memo-

---

F.Y.I.

Study Skills Tip

Making outlines is a handy way to stay focused on the main points. Outline the most important details of a subject you're studying, and fill in the specifics underneath each of these headings. Outlines are also easy to review with before a test.

rize and retain information before for a test.

Quick note: there are so many tips and tricks that work, and different ones work for different people. Here are only a few; talk to your friends or scour the internet for more suggestions. It's all a learning process.

Success is doing ordinary things extraordinarily well.

—Jim Rohn

DR. LISA SAYS...

When my students come to me with worries about studying for the test, I always say to them, "Try to think like me. What do I think is important for you to know? What did I spend a lot of time on in class that is also in the textbook?" Pretend you're the teacher. Look over your notes and the textbook. What concepts would you want the students to know? What questions would you ask? What answers would you look for? Another good strategy is to write questions as you do the reading. Then you'll have a study guide all ready for you when it comes time to study.

Flip It (Flashcards)

You may remember flashcards from your pre-school and kindergarten class. Boy, what fun they were. One side had a picture of a duck and the other side had a picture of a cartoon duck on it. Awesome.

Well, flashcards have applications beyond just helping you remember the names of barnyard animals. In fact, to meet the demand of teens for make-'em-yourself flashcards, office supply stores usually stock a nice selection of colorful index cards you can cut up – neon, pastel, lined, unlined. It's like art, in a way.

PARENT SPEAK

Parents can help their teens study by quizzing them using flashcards. Make sure you shuffle the flashcards and alternate between cards to ensure memorization.

F.Y.I.

Have a class that is the first or second in a series of classes you will be taking? For example, are you now taking Spanish I and plan on taking Spanish II next year? If so, laminate your flashcards at a local office supplies store so you could use them next year and the year after. It will save you loads of studying time in the next class!

So buy them, cut 'em up, and write all over them. You can use them to help you remember dates, places and names for your history classes, vocabulary words for your English classes, and formulas and theorems for your math classes.

Flashcards are also great because they're portable. Put a rubber band around them or put a hole through them and stick them on a metal ring. Pop them in your purse or in your back pocket, and you can whip them out for review anytime you find yourself standing in a line, waiting for a ride, or whenever you have a spare moment when your brain can be doing more than just sitting there in your head.

"The secret of success is consistency of purpose."

—Benjamin Disraeli

F.Y.I.

We live in a digital age, and it may be more your style to set up flashcards on your computer. Check out "The Flashcard Machine" at www.flashcardmachine.com

Own It (Mnemonic Devices)

Simply put, mnemonic devices are memory aids that you make up to help you remember details about the thing you're studying. Any memory improvement book or guide you'll ever seek out will have a chapter or two on effective mnemonic devices, and though we can't go on for pages and pages about them here, we can give you the gist of it.

A common mnemonic device is one you can use if you have to remember a list. You've probably had to learn the order for classifications of animal nomenclature in your biology or life science class. It goes: Kingdom, Phylum, Class, Order, Family Genus, Species. How do you remember it? Simple. Remember the sentence, "King Philip Came Over For Good Sausage" and you'll never mix up the order again.

It's not just clever sentences. You can think of rhymes, chants, phrases, abbreviations, and even images to help ingrain details in your mind as you're studying them. For example, when trying to remember whether an angle in math is acute or obtuse, just think to yourself that things are smaller are cuter, so an angle that is smaller than 90° is acute, and bigger than 90° is obtuse. And no one will ever forget the year Columbus discovered America, thanks to the person who came up with the mnemonic device:

"In fourteen hundred and ninety-two, Columbus sailed the ocean blue"

(1492, y'all)

Getting in the habit of creating your own mnemonic devices is a good thing. It makes the things you learn truly your own.

DR. LISA SAYS...

When making flashcards, take some time to put the information in your own words, rather than just copying it from the book or your notes. When you re-word the information, you think about it more deeply, which means that you will be more likely to remember it. To make flashcards even more useful, you can put a small clue or mnemonic on the bottom of the card. Cover the clue with your thumb while reviewing your flashcards, and reveal it if you need help. Again, this will help you think more deeply about the information, and you'll likely be able to remember the clue when you're struggling to remember something on the test.

"One must have strategies to execute dreams."

—Azim Premji

Stick it (Cramming)

FOOD FOR THOUGHT

According to a Penn State University article, people forget material because of "lack of familiar pattern, information overload, or information loss due to decay." Cramming does not allow the mind to establish a familiarity with the information and can even lead to forgetting information.

Cramming is a bad, bad thing if you're trying to learn things for the first time in the few minutes before a test. In that state of panic, you'll only be able to retain a few details that you might not even encounter in the scary moments to come.

True: you might luck out and those one or two things you crammed in there might actually show up. Cramming however, inevitably leads to details being quickly forgotten after the test is over because, after all, you didn't learn them

" I can accept failure but I can't accept not trying. "

——Michael Jordan

properly. It's better to learn right the first time so those details will be there for you on future tests, no?

It can be a good GOOD thing, however, if you take the last hour or few minutes before a test, to review your notes for important points or to refresh your memory on the finer details. Then not only have you learned everything, you're cementing them in place in your memory.

F.Y.I.

Test Taking Tip

Make sure to be on time to class (or maybe even a little early) on a test day. Nothing gets you off to a worse start to a test than running into class, heart pounding. You'll have to calm down before you can concentrate.

"We can do anything we want to do if we stick to it long enough."

—Helen Keller

Stuff It (Brain Food)

PARENT SPEAK

Parents can help students increase their concentration and performance on tests by making sure that healthy snacks are always available at home. Also, providing a balanced and nutritious breakfast and lunch for your child is a great way to ensure that they are attentive in school.

As we said, the brain is a highly metabolic organ. When you're thinking hard for extended periods of time, the neurons in your brain are firing messages back and forth and all over your body. The process is scientifically complicated, but the end result that we're concerned with here is that thinking really hard actually burns calories. Yup! On the level of about 1.5 calories a minute. Over the course of a day, your brain generally uses up 20%-25% pf all the energy you consume. So crack open that textbook and feel the burn.

"The King who cannot rule his diet will hardly rule his realm in peace and quiet."

—Unknown

To help support your brain function as it's getting its work out, you can see how the right fuel can provide a serious boost. Just like athletes who carbo-load before a big race or game, your brain is hungry for the right stuff to perform at its optimum. Keep a bowl or plate of snacks that are high in omega-3s and B-vitamins: eggs, nuts, wholegrains, salmon, sardines and tuna.

DR. LISA SAYS...

Understand the difference between recognition and recall. It is not enough to skim the chapter or your notes and feel like you know the information because you recognize the terms or names that are written down. It is quite different to cover up the information and make yourself say what is written there. When you try to recall without looking at your notes, you may find that you didn't know as much as you thought you did.

F.Y.I.

Did you know that water reduces stress hormones?

According to a health and wellness website, lifeshack,org, at least 80 ounces of water are needed to reduce stress hormones. Get hydrated!

Bring It — Developing Good

"Spectacular achievements are always preceded by painstaking preparation."

—Roger Staubach

S o you've studied your butt off, you've made notes, you've fed your brain, and you've gotten in some good zzz's. Now it's the day of the test, and it's time to show 'em all what you can do. It's time to bring your A-game.

Preparing for a test is most of the battle, and hopefully, you feel armed and ready as you go into the fray. But almost as important to your success as preparing for the test are your test-taking skills.

"What do you mean test-taking skills? Just sit down and fill in the right answers!" you may

---

F.Y.I.

Test Taking Tip

There's no harm in asking the teacher some specific questions about what will be covered on the test. The worst that can happen is he or she might say that they're not saying!

Test–Taking Skills

be saying to yourself. That's where you're mistaken!

On the day of the test, there are all kinds of ways you can trip yourself up so that the things you've studied aren't put to the best use. In a way, taking a test is a delicate balancing act between answering quickly, answering carefully, and answering completely. Let's look at the ways you can ensure your best performance on test day.

Success demands singleness of purpose.

—Vince Lombardi

PARENT SPEAK

Parents, make sure your teen gets a good night's rest before a test day. Attentiveness is a huge factor in test performance, and cramming till the wee hours may hurt more than it helps.

Chill (Relax)

FOOD FOR THOUGHT

A study conducted by the University of Michigan found that 1/3 of teens feel stressed out on a daily basis. The leading cause? The feeling of not being able to meet high expectations. Prolonged feelings of stress can lead to frustration, illness, aggression, and depression.

F reaking out. Flipping out. Spazzing. Call it what you want, but one thing's for sure: it's not a good thing to do during a test, although it certainly is easy to do!

Maybe you studied more than you've ever studied before and are psyching yourself out that it'll all be for nothing. Maybe you're encountering tougher questions than you expected. Maybe you're wondering if you maybe studied the wrong chapter!

In any case, it won't do you any good to go ballistic. When you're stressing out, you're not thinking clearly and you're more likely to second

"A problem is a chance for you to do your best."

—Duke Ellington

guess your answers and waste more time mulling them over than if you're confident and calm. So if you find yourself sweating under the collar, take a second to breathe deeply, focus, and chill out. It's the best thing you can do for yourself during a test.

F.Y.I.

A few simple ways to manage stress:

1. Positive "Self-Talk" : Try repeating to yourself silently "I can handle this" or "It's going to be O.K." Having a positive attitude can make stress dissapear.

2. See the funny side of life! Look at your situation from a comical perspective and you'll be able to relax, and when you're relaxed you can think more clearly.

DR. LISA SAYS...

When you get the test, take a minute to empty out everything that is cluttering up your brain before you look at any of the questions. Write down all of your mnemonics, formulas, or information that you're afraid that you'll forget or get confused about. This will not only serve as practical help, but it will also calm you down by focusing you on the information, not on the difficulty of the test. You'll see how much you really do know, and you'll be able to tackle the questions with confidence.

IDK (Guess)

If, despite your best studying efforts, you come across a question that you just don't know the answer to, you'll have to resort to guessing. Guessing, however, isn't an entirely random act that leaves you to chance. There are smart ways to guess that'll greatly improve the probability that you'll do it correctly.

If it's a multiple choice question, you'll want to go through and eliminate any obviously incorrect answers. It helps to physically draw a line or an x through them so you focus on the few choices you have left. If you can eliminate enough to 2 have answer choices, go with your instinct. If you studied well enough, the answer is hidden somewhere in your memory and the surest way to fish it out is to just go with your gut. Second-guessing wastes time, and may cause you to reason yourself out of the right answer.

If the question requires a written answer, there's really nothing you can do but to write about what you do know with such conviction that it's a little less noticeable that you don't really know the exact and direct answer to what's being asked of you. Unfortunately, there's not much else you can do in this scenario!

And finally, if you are forced to guess on a multiple choice test because you're running low on time, here's something you should know: Probability shows that you are more likely to get more questions correct if you are randomly guessing with ONE letter instead of picking a different letter each time. Basically, if you have 5 questions left and 5 seconds on the clock, pick a letter and commit. D's all the way down! A column of C's! It doesn't matter which letter, just pick one and stick with it.

And hope for the best!

TIME CRUNCH

How would you manage your time in the following situation?

You're staring at an impossible test, given to you by one of your more annoying teachers. It has 30 multiple choice questions, 5 short answers… and, for the topper: an essay.

The best thing about this mess is, there's only an hour to complete the whole thing.

So how much time do you spend…

Answering the M.C. questions you do know?_____
Guessing on the M.C. questions you don't know?_____
Answering the short answers?_____
Writing the essay? _____
Freaking out? _____

And while we're at it, what order would you do it all in?

Cover Your Butt (Check Your Answers)

Y ou know from experience: the worst of the incorrect answers you find on a test that's been graded and handed back to you are the ones you lost points on because of carelessness even though you knew the answers.

There are different ways you can miss your mark. You can read questions incorrectly or hastily. You can accidentally fill in or write in the wrong answer. You can circle the right answer... but on the wrong question! You can pick the wrong answer

FOOD FOR THOUGHT

If you take tests on answer sheets that are graded by a machine, make sure you erase and fill in very carefully. Sometimes, even if you answer a question right but do not erase another answer completely, you will get marked wrong. So be careful and keep a good eraser handy at all times!

" If you think you can, you can. And if you think you can't, you're right. "

——Henry Ford

because you didn't read through all of the choices (and if you had, you would have found a better answer than the one you picked).

For all of the above and more, it's important to check your answers, but only if you have time. For most tests, it's wiser to get through to the end and then use the remaining time to cover your butt, rather than to worry and fret and waste time by going through each question you complete twice.

F.Y.I.

Test Taking Tip

When going back over your answers, only change answers if you find that you misread or misinterpreted the question. Why? Because it's usually the case that the first answer that you were compelled to put down is the correct one.

Most people give up just when they're about to achieve success. They quit on the one-yard line. They give up at the last minute of the game, one foot from a winning touchdown.

—Ross Perot

Tick Tock (Be Aware of Time Limits)

FOOD FOR THOUGHT

When taking standardized tests, testing can last up to five hours with only one or two breaks. To rest your hands, eyes, and brain, try to take 20 second breaks every 15 minutes or so to keep you fresh and going.

The ticking clock is your nastiest opponent when you're taking a timed test. You could know every answer to every question on a test, and never get to prove it because you're cut short. That's why it's important to be aware of your time limit throughout the duration of the test.

If the test is for one of your classes and is composed of different types of questions (a mix of multiple choice, matching, fill-in's and essays, for example) it's good to always start out by taking

"No man is ever whipped until he quits – in his own mind."

—Napoleon Hill

a minute or so to get the lay of the land. Flip through the test and make sure there isn't a massive essay question on the very last page.

If it is a multiple choice test, do a quick calculation in your head. If you've got 30 questions and 60 minutes to complete the test, you'll know you should only be spending roughly 2 minutes on each question. If one question has sucked up 4 minutes and you still don't have the answer, it's time to guess!

In short, pace yourself. Keep an eye on the clock, and know that you can beat it.

F.Y.I.

Test Taking Tip

Bring your own watch to a timed test and keep it on your desk in plain view of the teacher. It's better if it's digital so you can get the read on it at-a-glance. Having to look up at a wall clock over and over and counting up the time you have left is a good way to waste precious minutes.

> Perseverance is the hard work you do after you get tired of doing the hard work you already did.
> ——Newt Gingrich

Me Time – Relaxing and

If you've committed yourself to doing well on a test, then you know how easy it is to get carried away. Have you ever woken up on the day of the test feeling like you were beaten up in your sleep, and then realized that it's because you've only gotten 3 hours of it? Have you ever been up after an evening at a desk only to feel like you need to sit down again... and then realized it's because you've forgotten to eat dinner?

F.Y.I.

According to a Penn State University article, here are some Do's and Don'ts when dealing with test anxiety:

✓ Don't stay up late studying the night before. You need the sleep. Begin studying a week in advance if possible.

✓ Don't spend time with classmates who generate stress for you on test day.

✓ Don't take those last few moments before the test for last minute cramming. Try to relax and spend that time reading the newspaper or some other distraction.

✓ Do remind yourself that the test is only a test.

✓ Do focus on integrating details into main ideas.

✓ Do reward yourself after the test with food or a movie or some other treat.

✓ Do something relaxing the last hour before the test.

✓ Do tell yourself that you will do your best on the test, and that will be enough!

Not Overdoing It

Have you ever sat down to take a test and realized that none of the answers are coming to you? "But why? I've spent every waking moment over the last week studying for this stupid thing!"

The key is "me time." You need it. Your brain is a powerful thing, but it needs time to rest if it's going to do you proud on the big day. Your body is the vehicle for your brain, but it too can break down at a critical moment if you haven't been good to it.

Here are some tips for keeping both your brain and your body happy so that they don't rebel on test day.

FOOD FOR THOUGHT

It is estimated that around 10 percent of all teens suffer from an anxiety disorder.

Great works are performed not by strength but by perseverance.

—Samuel Johnson

Zoom Out (Pacing Yourself)

FOOD FOR THOUGHT

One major advantage of beginning to study at least a week in advance is that you can ask more questions in class. If you start studying the night before, anything you don't understand will probably go unanswered and become a source of anxiety while taking the test.

If you've made a good study schedule in preparation for a test, then you're probably good in this category. Still, it bears repeating that in your studies, you're going to retain the most information if you make sure you pace yourself and schedule in breaks so your brain can take a breather.

Studies vary in their findings on how long the brain can effectively concentrate in one sitting, but it's generally understood that there's a definite limit to how much it can take. Common sense tells you that you're going to be more

"Motivation is what gets you started. Habit is what keeps you going!"

—Jim Ryun

capable of understanding and retaining the things you read in the first hour of studying than you are in the sixth hour of studying (if you've been studying the whole time).

Be realistic with yourself. If you look at your study schedule and it says, "Monday: study 10 chapters of history. Tuesday: study 8 more chapters, review previous 10 chapters," you're probably setting yourself up for major failure.

Start studying early enough in the week to give yourself enough time to cover all the material at a reasonable pace before a test, and you'll be okay. Give yourself plenty of notice for an upcoming test, and make the best use of the time you've got without overdoing it.

DR. LISA SAYS...

Consider the idea that it's okay to not be perfect in every single thing that you do. Other than high school, there is no other time in your life where you are expected to excel in every subject. In college, you pick a major after your first year or two. If you go to grad school, you specialize further in an even smaller topic. Once you get a job, you may be an expert in your field, but you won't be an expert on everything. So don't be too hard on yourself if you don't get 100% on every test in every class.

Zone Out (Taking Breaks)

FOOD FOR THOUGHT

Different frequencies and durations work for different people. Some people prefer to take 5 minute breaks every 30-minutes, while others like to do two hours followed by a 30-minute break. There's no optimal number. See which works best for you!

So you've scheduled out and set aside time to get serious about your studying. Have you scheduled in your breaks?

Basically, if you're settling in for a long one-on-one time with the ol' books, it's a good policy to give yourself regularly-scheduled breaks. After every hour of studying, stand up to stretch your legs, close your eyes to give them a rest, get a cup of juice or refill your snack bowl, and just generally reward yourself for the work you've done so far.

It's easy to let your breaks get the better of you, however, so make sure you set an end-time for each of them. If you stand up after an hour of

The road to success is dotted with many tempting parking places.

—Unknown

studying and decide that you're going to play a video game "for a while," you might find at the end of the night that you've spent an hour studying, and 3 hours getting to the end of the level. The monster or boss may be defeated, but your open textbook is not vanquished!

Take breaks, but control them. Then, when you're ready, jump right back in—refreshed and recharged!

F.Y.I.

Here are some more study break ideas to help you relax:

Take a brisk walk or jog, watch a funny movie or episode from your favorite TV show (depending on how long your break is), read something for fun that's not related to school, or make a fun and delicious snack.

DR. LISA SAYS...

Make sure to get some exercise. Not only will it keep you healthy, but it is also a much better method for staying alert than caffeine or energy drinks. If you're feeling drowsy during a study session, or if you find it hard to get started, try taking a 15-minute walk around the block, or running up and down the stairs for 10 minutes. Ideas for multitasking include taking your flashcards out while you stroll around the neighborhood, downloading book chapters onto your iPod to listen to while lifting weights, or propping your notes up on the elliptical machine at the gym.

Zonk Out (Importance of Sleep)

FOOD FOR THOUGHT

A study that appeared in the medical journal Pediatrics pointed out that based on the average start time for school, teens were losing 2 hours of needed sleep each weekday. The study also found lower alertness in the morning compared to the afternoon because of this grogginess.

You've heard that you need at least 8 hours of sleep, right? Well some studies have shown that that number is actually even higher for teens, who are biologically driven to need more! You may need 9 or 10 hours!

Chances are, however, that your schedule—with school, your extracurriculars, and your sports and hobbies—won't allow you to catch quite that many zzz's. And since you can't very well march into the school office and demand that they start classes much later, for now it's enough to be aware that you should be getting as much sleep as possible, especially the night before a big test.

Sleepiness produces poor concentration and inattentiveness. What good is studying hard for a test if on the day you take it, you have to read

"Health is the first muse, and sleep is the condition to produce it."

—Ralph Waldo Emerson

each question twice to understand it, and then can't even finish before the time runs out? Not getting enough sleep also adversely affects your memory, so all the things you took the time to read and take notes on might be lost to a thing as silly as tiredness.

Avoid these dangers and hit the hay when your body starts showing the signs of sleepiness. How much sleep do you need, you may ask? Here's a simple way to figure it out: If you're tired... you need more!

F.Y.I.

Are you an athlete or a part of the speech and debate team at school? Do you not get home till late in the evening? Maybe you could use study hall or the library before practice starts to get some homework done. Do you travel on the bus to games? Study your flashcards on the way to the game. Time management is essential to success and allows you to get more sleep!

> "Four steps to achievement: plan purposefully, prepare prayerfully, proceed positively, pursue persistently."
>
> —William A. Ward

The Big Ones—Standardizec

> "Spectacular achieve- ment is always pre- ceded by spectacular prepara- tion."
>
> —Robert H. Schuller

Tests for your classes at school can be daunt- ing and can stress you out, but the good news is, there are a lot of them. Screwing up on a test here or there isn't going to tank your grade or significantly affect your chances of getting into college.

F.Y.I.

According to a popular web survey conducted in 2005, it was discovered that teens take a gen- erally positive view toward standardized testing.

✓ 57% say there is about the right amount of emphasis on testing

✓ 47% say the need to cover material for stan- dardized tests positively affects the way their teachers use classroom time (and only 20% say it has a negative effect).

Findings from the 37th Annual Phi Delta Kappa/ Gallup Poll of the Public's Attitudes Toward the Public Schools, released on Aug. 23 in Washing- ton, D.C.

Tests

This alphabet soup of exams can seem over-whelming, intimidating, and life-altering, but by learning about each exam, what they test, how they test, and how to best prepare for it, you can ease some of that anxiety before test day.

The stakes are raised considerably higher on standardized tests however. You may already be well aware of the ones looming on your horizon: the PSATs, your AP tests, and the dreaded SATs.

The PSATs, SATs, and AP tests are issued by the Educational Testing Service (ETS) and the College Board. You may think that they were created to make your life a living hell and to make sure you stay stressed out all the way to your senior year, but what they're really here for is to level out the playing field. Let's take a look at the tests that you and the rest of the country will have to be subjected to... er... will have to experience, together.

PARENT SPEAK

Get involved in the test preparation process. Help students find a test-prep style that works for them and encourage them along the way.

The PSAT

The PSAT, or Preliminary SAT is a multiple-choice test that serves primarily as a practice for the real SATs, and also as a test to determine eligibility for the National Merit Scholarship Program. For that reason, it's also sometimes referred to as the NMSQT (National Merit Scholarship Qualifying Test).

The PSAT is taken mostly by high school sophomores and juniors, but in recent years has also been taken by 8th and even 7th graders. The PSAT is really your best chance to see what the SAT looks like, feels like, and gauge in which areas you need improvement in. The sooner you take it, the more time you have to prepare for the real exam, and the better you'll feel going into it.

It's a funny thing, the more I practice the luckier I get.

—Arnold Palmer

The test is composed of three sections: mathematics, critical reading, and writing. It takes two hours and ten minutes to complete, with the points adding up to a total of 240.

Though this test is not very important in affecting your admission into college, doing well on it can certainly help you score some scholarships, rack up some National Merit honors, and look impressive to college admissions officers when it's listed on your transcript.

To learn more about the PSAT, visit www.ets.org for more information.

"Taking the PSAT helped me feel more confident when I took the SAT. I got to see how the test works without feeling the pressure."

F.Y.I.

What is the National Merit Scholarship, and why would you want it? You can learn what it is, how to qualify, and what the benefits to your college career are by visiting www.nationalmerit.org.

AP Tests

The Advanced Placement (AP) Program is a program that offers college-level courses in various subjects in high schools across the country. If you're studying for an AP Test, it's most likely because you're currently enrolled in an AP class at your school (although you don't need to be enrolled in a class to take the test).

There are over 30 subjects in which you can take AP courses, all of which culminate on a major test day where you put what you've learned to use on a long and comprehensive exam (the format of which varies depending on the subject).

Tests are scored on a scale of 1 to 5, 1 being "No Recommendation" and 5 being "Extremely well-qualified". Any score of 3 and above will count towards college credit – meaning you won't have to take those courses in college.

People elect to take AP courses in high school for a number of reasons, the most common being to challenge themselves, to save themselves the trouble of taking the classes in college (and therefore saving on tuition), and to show college admissions officers that they are intelligent and motivated. Even though a poor AP score won't necessarily adversely affect your chances of getting into college, doing well on AP courses and tests and taking a number of them can make you a major contender when admission time rolls around.

F.Y.I.

As of 2008, the following are the AP courses and tests available to high school students:

Art History	Italian Language and Culture
Biology	Japanese Language and Culture
Calculus AB	Latin Literature
Calculus BC	Latin: Virgil
Chemistry	Macroeconomics
Chinese Language and Culture	Microeconomics
Computer Science A	Music Theory
Computer Science AB	Physics B
English Language and Composition	Physics C: Electricity and Magnetism
English Literature and Composition	Psychology
Environmental Science	Spanish Language
European History	Spanish Literature
French Language	Statistics
French Literature	Studio Art: 2-D Design
German Language	Studio Art: 3-D Design
Government and Politics: Comparative	Studio Art: Drawing
Government and Politics: United States	United States History
Human Geography	World History

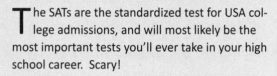

The SAT – Math

The SATs are the standardized test for USA college admissions, and will most likely be the most important tests you'll ever take in your high school career. Scary!

There are many ways to prepare for the math portion of the SAT including, test prep books, classes, and individual tutors. You could even ask your teachers for some extra worksheets to keep your mind fresh on the many math topics that are tested (and score some bonus points with them too!).

The test itself takes about 4 hours to complete and is made up of groups of questions that fall into the category of "critical reading," "mathematics," and writing. Scores range from a possible 600 to 2400, combining the results from the three different 800-point sections. It's offered at special testing centers in every major city many times each month, so you don't have to sign up to take it until you're ready.

The mathematics section consists of one 25-minute section of multiple choice questions, one 25-minute section with a combination of multiple choice questions and fill-in (grid-in) questions, and one 20-minute section of all multiple choice questions. The questions test you on your knowledge and skill with numbers and operations, algebra and functions, geometry, statistics, probability, and data analysis.

Thankfully, it is relatively easy to familiarize yourself with the types of questions asked on the math section – more so than on the verbal section. Practice, practice, and more practice at these, using of test prep materials, can help you boost your potential score in this section by many tens of points if you're willing to put in the time and effort.

F.Y.I.

How many high school students received a perfect score on the SATs in 2006?

238, or approximately .016% of the 1.5 million students who took it, according to College Board.

> "Do not worry about your problems with mathematics, I assure you mine are far greater."
>
> —Albert Einstein

The SAT – Verbal (Critical Reading a

FOOD FOR THOUGHT

One of the common answers teachers give when asked how students should get read for the SAT is, "Start reading ten years ago." Reading is a skill you've been sharpening all your life — keep it up by reading things that interest you (magazines, detective novels, science fiction, non-fiction, whatever) and stretches your vocabulary.

A little more tricky to master are the critical reading and writing sections.

The critical reading section consists of two 25-minute sections and one 20-minute section, and is composed of sentence completion questions and reading comprehension questions (based on writing passages you'll read on the test). This section tests both your comprehension skills and your vocabulary level. It's usually the questions that require knowledge of complex vocabulary that proves challenging for most teens and students. Get a leg up on the conversation by starting to prepare for this early, and making flashcards to test yourself on words.

The writing section includes multiple choice questions and a short essay. The multiple choice questions include error identification questions, sentence improvement questions, and paragraph improvement questions—basically testing for your knowledge of grammar rules and usage. The essay is 25 minutes long and is based on a prompt you are given which is usually broad and philosophical. There is no set structure for the

/riting)

essay; you can write it any way you want as long as you use examples taken from your reading, studies, experience, or observations to support your argument.

For more information on this test, visit www.collegeboard.com

TIME CRUNCH

How would you manage your time in the following situation?

It's a week before your scheduled SAT, and you're stressing out majorly. You have all your vocabulary flashcards, but you haven't studied them. You have two test-prep books filled with practice questions that you haven't done, but you know you must. On top of studying for SATs, you've got your regular school workload.

How much time do you spend each day…

Doing regular school homework? _____
Studying for the SATs? _____
Relaxing? _____
Doing your other extracurricular activities? _____
Sleeping? _____

Ninja Training! – Standar

> When you're prepared, you're more confi-dent. When you have a strat-egy, you're more com-fortable.
>
> —Fred Couples, American golfer

So you now know the SAT is the BIG ONE. Don't panic too much, little grasshopper. You, too, can become an SAT master. Instead of letting your competition stress you out, let it push you to study harder and prepare better than ever before.

And truthfully, if you don't get there as quickly as you need to and you don't get the score you want, you can always take the test again. Check with the college of your choice, however. Some colleges will only consider your top score, while others will want to take all your scores into

F.Y.I.

Across the nation, education experts are engaged in an ongoing debate over whether or not the SATs actually measure intelligence and a student's ability to succeed. But while the argument rages, it's clear that colleges are placing more and more emphasis on SAT performance as an admission criteria. More teens apply to college every year and it gets more competitive.

zed Test Prep

consideration. In any case, it's probably a good idea to take it very seriously each and every time you attempt it, and go into the arena prepared to perform like a pro.

Even though it's a "standardized test," and is supposed to level out the playing field and put everyone on an equal footing, that's simply not the case. Teens across the country are practicing their SAT-taking skills, and many of them are getting the extra help incognito (they aren't mentioning it to their friends). It's a nationwide test, so in a way, everyone's your competition, after all!

So are you ready to train? Step into the dojo and get ready to flex your mind-muscle.

DR. LISA SAYS...

The best way to prep for standardized tests is to do practice questions, practice questions, and more practice questions. Keep a notebook filled with sections like vocabulary words that you need to know and math problems (with detailed solutions) that you missed. Review the information in the notebook on a regular basis. If you do this enough, you'll start to see some very familiar questions repeated in different ways. As for the essay, the questions are often fairly broad. In your notebook, keep outlines of 4-5 essays from the practice tests. You'll probably be able to use at least one of these essays on the test, with only minor adaptations necessary in order to fit the specific question.

The Dojo (Test Prep Classes)

FOOD FOR THOUGHT

Shop around for an SAT preparation class or tutor within your budget that works with your schedule. They can range from several hundred dollars to a few thousand dollars, and can range in intensity from weekly to daily classes.

The biggest evidence that this "standardized test" isn't actually testing everyone on a level playing field is the existence of many, many different test prep classes that are available to help you meet your SAT-scoring goals. Though many places double as tutoring centers, they do much of their business training students whose parents can pay the tuition to master the art of SAT-taking.

If this is the way you want to go, know that much of your ultimate success on the SAT depends not only on attending this type of class, but also on your willingness to do the extra homework and practice tests regularly as well as your regular

"Success is where preparation and opportunity meet."

——Bobby Unser

school workload. For the period of time you're taking the course, you may be forced to cut out some of your sports or extracurricular commitments.

An internet search will quickly turn up the SAT test-prep courses in your area that will work for you and your schedule. Kaplan is one of the most reputable of the test preparation academies and has classes enrolling in cities across the country. Visit www.kaplan.com to check them out.

" Today's preparation determines tomorrow's achieve- ment. "

—Unknown

F.Y.I.

Knowing your learning style will help you pick the program that most fits your abilities and needs. Not sure what your style is? Ask your teachers for learning styles resources, or try taking an online inventory test like the one at www.learning-styles-online.com

Secret Teachings (Test Prep Books)

FOOD FOR THOUGHT

Using test prep books instead of taking a class doesn't mean you have to go solo – hit the books with a friend! You can take turns quizzing each other on vocab words, work through tough problems together, and split the costs of the books themselves so you have some celebration cash left over after testing season's done.

If being self-taught in the art of test-prep is more your style (and more within your family's budget), a quick visit to your local bookstore will uncover a trove of resources in the test preparation section.

Many different publishers offer a number of preparation books. That may take different approaches to preparing you, but all will feature plenty of practice exams and questions, along with test-taking tips and tricks.

The key to success with test-prep books and guides is discipline. When you're setting your own pace and intensity, it's easy to slack off, and harder to monitor your progress. You need to be your own taskmaster if you choose this approach. Set aside some time every day to devote to SAT prep. Create lists of vocabulary words and math formulas to review over and over.

Taking your destiny into your own hands is a challenge that you'll have to meet head on. Time to crack open those books, and crack that whip!

If you think that test prep books are the way to

go, but are worried about staying on track and motivated, create a schedule for yourself and build in rewards when you meet your goals. For example, after you've studied your vocabulary flash cards and reviewed your formulas, take a practice exam and see how you did. Even if you didn't get the score you were hoping for, take a break doing something other than study for a day. Then hit the books again, ready to take on the challenge! Pacing yourself and rewarding yourself with a little time off is the only way you can get through something as massive as SAT prep.

F.Y.I.

Here are some reputable publishers of test-preparation books to check out:
✓ Kaplan
✓ Princeton Review
✓ Grubers
✓ Acro Masters
The College Board also publishes an official study guide for the SAT that you can get in most bookstores.

" All good is hard. All evil is easy. Dying, losing, cheating, and mediocrity is easy. Stay away from easy. "

—Scott Alexander

What NOT To Do – Chea

If you think about all the effort that would go into cheating and the huge risk of having cheating go wrong, wouldn't it make more sense to just put that effort into studying? Yes, SATs are important… but they're not THAT important!

There's an entire world of reasons teens are pressured or lured into cheating for the first time, and to continue cheating after that. You may feel the need to please your parents, but feel less than confident about your own intellect. You may see or suspect your friends of doing better than you, and not know how to catch up without using methods that are less than honest.

Cheating on tests at school is bad enough, and comes with dire consequences, but cheating on standardized test is a big, big no-no, and something that can get you barred from entrance into

F.Y.I.

Common punishments for cheating at school:

✓ A failing grade
✓ Detention
✓ Suspension
✓ Phone call to parents
✓ Mark on your permanent record

ng

ALL colleges. Though there are moral and philosophical arguments against cheating, let's just say it out loud: the most convincing deterrent to cheating is knowing what will happen to you if you do it. And though that's not a fun thing to discuss, knowing is important if you want to effectively talk yourself out of getting involved in a bad situation.

The consequences you face when caught cheating clearly outweigh any benefit you may have thought you were getting by doing it, as you will see in plentiful example here. Read on!

> Discipline is the bridge between goals and accomplishment.
>
> —Jim Rohn

FOOD FOR THOUGHT

When faced with a difficult challenge in school, make a to-do list of all the things you can do to tackle it head on. List the resources you can use to study, like books or notes. Also think about the people you can go to for help, your teacher or a tutor. Then think of different ways to study like making your own exam or pairing up with a friend to quiz each other. Remember, teaching is the best way to really learn something!

Red-Handed (Academic Consequences)

L et's cut to the chase.

Your junior high or high school likely has some pretty harsh punishments for cheating on tests. You could be facing hours of detention when you have much better things to do with your time. That disciplinary action for cheating on your academic record won't make things easy for you for a good long while, as we'll discuss here soon enough.

HALL OF SHAME

In 2008, six sopho-mores at Harvard-Westlake—a prestigious, top-per-forming Los Angeles private school— were expelled and more than a dozen other students faced suspensions when it was discovered they conspired and stole Spanish and history midterm tests and passed them around.

"Keep your dreams alive. Understand to achieve anything requires faith and belief in yourself, vision, hard work, determination, and dedication. Remember all things are possible for those who believe."

—Gail Devers

Taking a longer view however, cheating on tests literally cheats you out of the knowledge that should be rightfully yours. While others are learning and retaining information in a way that will allow them to use it to score better on standardized tests and be more effective and intelligent communicators, you'll have deprived yourself of the learning process, and for something as insignificant in the long run as a better score or letter grade.

PARENT SPEAK

Talk to your child about cheating. Some students feel the need to cheat because they feel pressured to do well on exams — ease that pressure by encouraging them in their studies and showing them how to weigh the consequences of cheating.

DR. LISA SAYS...

To me, the worst consequence of cheating is that in the long run, you don't learn the information. You are setting yourself up to be less knowledgeable than your classmates who really did study, and you're handicapping yourself for when you have to compete in college. Putting aside the idea of competing with others, think about all the information that you're depriving yourself of. Life is much more interesting and fulfilling when you understand a lot about the world in which you live. And as my 7th grade math teacher used to say, "it's better to be smart because smart people get more jokes, so they get to laugh more."

They're Onto You (Ramifications for College

If it's still not clear why getting caught cheating can really mess you up, get ready. Here comes the doozy.

One of the biggest, if not the biggest red flags on a student record that prompts colleges to bypass an applicant is a history of cheating. The reason for this is that colleges want to turn out students who are prepared to do their own scholarship

HALL OF SHAME

In 2007, thirty-four students at the prestigious Duke University business administration school were found guilty of cheating on a take-home test. 9 were expelled, 15 were suspended for a whole year, and 9 were failed from the course. Only 4 were cleared of the charges altogether.

> I was thrown out of college for cheating on the metaphysics exam; I looked into the soul of the boy next to me.
>
> —Woody Allen

and contribute original ideas to the field. Plagiarism is the ultimate no-no in every college class, and the most obvious predictor of a college plagiarist is a high school cheater.

So if you still think that cheating is no big deal, consider for a moment that to colleges, it is a very big deal, and then decide whose opinion might mean a little bit more when it comes to your future.

THE BASICS

plagiarism

n. 1. The unauthorized use or close imitation of the language and thoughts of another author and the representation of them as one's own original work. 2. Something used and represented in this manner.

Definition from dictionary.com

"Pretty much any teacher or college professor will tell you that it's better to ask for help and try your best than to cheat. You can always try harder on your next test, but it's much harder to regain someone's trust."

Can't Shake It (Social Consequences)

FOOD FOR THOUGHT

Why do so many teens think that cheating is no big deal? In 200, the Josephson's Institute of Ethics found that 34% of teens said their parents never talked to them about cheating.

Getting caught cheating sucks for many reasons, and on top of all of those, there are the social consequences. When you're worried about getting that good grade at all costs, what your friends will think of you may be the last thing on your mind. How would you feel, however, if you knew that one of your classmates got a better grade on an test than you did after cheating? Angry, right? Now imagine that the cheater is you.

Cheating can cost you friendships—both the ones you have and the ones you would have made if you didn't have a reputation as a cheater. Few people want to risk their own credibility by being associated with a known cheater (would they be implicated as an accomplice if you're caught in a cheating scheme, they might wonder), and no one wants to run the risk of being pressured to

"Don't trust the person who has broken faith once."

—William Shakespeare

give up hard-earned test or homework notes and answers.

And if you think your teachers are above gossip, think again. Just as most people would, they warn each other about cheaters they've caught and they brag about how they caught them. If you think your classes are hard now, think of how hard they'll be when the teacher has a bad impression of you and your work from the very beginning.

You've heard that people's reputations precede them. When you're a cheater, this truism spells major, major disaster.

> "To be trusted is a greater compliment than being loved."
>
> —George MacDonald

DR. LISA SAYS...

Even if you don't get caught, the knowledge that you cheated will be with you forever. In a way, this is the worst consequence because you will always be questioning if you really deserve the things that you have gotten. You'll wonder what would have happened if you had tried to make it through without cheating. You will feel insecure about yourself and begin to doubt your abilities. You will start to think that you can't do anything on your own, and you'll begin to rely on cheating as a crutch.

Pwned! – Dealing Witl

> Courage doesn't always roar. Sometimes courage is the quiet voice at the end of the day saying, 'I will try again tomorrow.'
>
> —Mary Anne Radmacher

To your knowledge, you've done everything right. You studied hard, you took notes, you paced yourself, and you resisted the temptation to cheat. But you took that test and the results were... well, they weren't great.

What now?

Failure is hard to deal with, and because humans are thinking, feeling beings, it's hard not to analyze and overanalyze a failure, especially one

F.Y.I.

Check out these famous "failures" who didn't let a rough start get them down:

✓ Bill Gates dropped out of Harvard University before founding Microsoft and becoming the world's richest man.

✓ Abraham Lincoln was defeated in eight political campaigns before becoming elected as the 16th president of the United States.

Failure

that you feel was undeserved. Teens, especially, are hard on themselves.

But before you let one dismal grade make you depressed and gloomy, take a moment to look on the bright side of failure. There's a bright side, we promise, and in fact, a "failure" could be anything but that when looked at logically.

"Failure is the condiment that gives success its flavor."

——Truman Capote

DR. LISA SAYS...

Fear of failure can be a major motivator for many high achievers. Some people will do anything to avoid looking stupid, since school can start to look like a never-ending game where you're only as smart as your next test. However, failing one test (or even getting a dreaded B or C) is not the worst thing in the world. You won't be perfect at every single thing you do every day for the rest of your life, and the earlier that you see that doing less than stellar on one exam is not the end of the world, the less afraid you will be of failure in the future. You'll be free to just concentrate on the work itself.

Fool Me Once – (Learning From Mistakes)

You know that Thomas Edison didn't just stick some wire and some glass together and invent the lightbulb in one shot, right? No, he tried and failed hundreds of times, and some of his attempts were absolutely ridiculous, by his own admission. But every so-called "failure" took him a step closer to discovering the right combination, and now generations of people all over the world have benefited from his gumption.

So too, should you regard any of your poor test scores. They shouldn't be lamented, dismissed, or forgotten. There are important lessons to be

FOOD FOR THOUGHT

Test Taking Tip

If your teacher is offering a review session after school, go to it. They may give out some valuable clues about what's going to be on the test as a reward for people who took the extra time to attend.

> I have not failed. I've just found 10,000 ways that won't work.
>
> —Thomas Edison

gleaned from those tests you haven't performed up to snuff on. Were your errors a result of poor preparation, or a focus on the wrong material? Were you tired going into the test?

One bad test score here or there isn't going to ruin you, but a careful consideration of what went wrong and an assessment of what needs to be improved for next time can certainly help you.

> "The successful man will profit from his mistakes and try again in a different way."
> —Dale Carnegie

DR. LISA SAYS...

I was always one of those self-punishing overachievers. I would beat myself up for days over getting a 98% on an exam because I thought that any score less than an A+ on every single quiz or test would completely blow my chance for success. During my freshman year of college, I got a D on my first test in cognitive psychology. When I called home in hysterics, my father's response was, "Wonderful. It's good for you." I hung up on him. But he was right – I needed to learn to deal with it and move on. And guess what? Despite a few low test grades here and there, I still ended up with a Ph.D. from a great school and a job that I love.

Zeroing In – (Identifying Weaknesses)

FOOD FOR THOUGHT

It's not always your bad. When you get a test back with a dissatisfactory score, spend the first few minutes to check if there are grading mistakes, and/or errors in addition on your score.

So here it is in your hand: a test that you're not too proud of. It's time to take it apart. No, not literally (if you've begun the ripping, get out the scotch tape)! It's time to see it for its component parts and see where you went wrong. As you look at the incorrect answers, ask yourself the following questions.

• Was it a careless error? Did you actually know what the correct answer was, or could you have figured it out with a little less haste?

• Did you miss questions because you were hurrying? Was the time restriction a problem? Could it be fixed with better pacing?

"If it is a mistake of the head and not the heart don't worry about it, that's the way we learn."

——Earl Warren

• Did you focus on the wrong things when studying? Were you too narrow in your focus? Too broad?

• Is there a way you can take notes that will be more effective in helping you remember the right details? What more or LESS should you be doing to prepare yourself optimally for another test of this type/for this class?

• Did you get enough sleep? Did you have enough to eat? Were you feeling healthy? Calm? Prepared? Confident?

> Don't spend your time beating yourself up about mistakes you made. Making mistakes is how you learn – I always remember the answers to the questions I get wrong, not the ones I get right.

F.Y.I.

Eating right and getting enough sleep really do affect how you'll do on a test! Try to eat some protein the morning of your test and be sure to stay hydrated so you can focus on what you've learned and not your parched throat or growling stomach.

Patching Up – (Fixing Weaknesses)

FOOD FOR THOUGHT

If you're having trouble in a class, chances are that other students are struggling, too. Finding a few classmates or friends who have similar questions may make it less intimidating to ask for help.

The above questions should help you identify the areas you might need to make necessary adjustments before the next test. Remember that improving your test-taking skills is an ongoing process. You won't perfect it in one try, even if you correctly identify all of your weaknesses every single time.

When you're making adjustments and your test scores still aren't getting any better, it's always a good idea to get a second opinion or enlist some help. Talk to the teacher who's administering the killer tests and see if he/she is willing to give you

"Learn from the mistakes of others. You can't live long enough to make them all yourself."

——Martin Vanbee

some pointers on what to focus on, or see if he/she will point out to you what you're doing wrong. It can't hurt to let him/her know you care about your scores and you're serious about raising them.

Also remember that different teachers have different testing styles. Starting a new class can throw you for a loop if the type of test the teacher administers isn't what you're used to. Persistence, vigilence, and assessment will get you where you want to be, or at least closer to hitting your mark.

F.Y.I.

Test Taking Tip

You don't learn from your mistakes unless you understand what you did wrong. Don't be shy about arranging to meet with your teacher to discuss the questions you got wrong, or about asking your classmates to see what their answers were if they got them right and you didn't.

"There are no foolish questions and no man becomes a fool until he has stopped asking questions."

—Charles P. Steinmetz

'Til the Fat Lady Sings – (Don't Give Up)

Y ou may bomb one test. You may bomb the next time, and the time after that. But sooner or later, your hard work will pay off and you'll get both the score you want and the score you deserve.

Don't give up if your progress isn't as speedy as you want it to be, and don't stop looking for ways to speed up your progress! Figuring out the right combinations of test-preparation methods and test-taking skills for all the different kinds of tests you will encounter can be a art and a craft that takes years to perfect.

FOOD FOR THOUGHT

If a poor test score is really going to hurt your grade, consider asking the teacher for a make-up exam, or for extra credit opportunities. It's always a good thing to show him/ her that you're seri-ous about doing well in the class.

"Never, never, never quit!"

——Winston Churchill

If life is supposed to be a journey and not just a destination, then preparing and taking the SAT's is one of the parts of your life that can teach you a lot about yourself and give you many valuable lessons, along with a great vocabulary!

Everything you've put into it you're going to take with you to college, into the workplace and beyond. The same skills and behaviors you learn to ace tests will help you face many challenges beyond the academic. So chin up, chest out, and look ahead!

THE BASICS

perseverance

n. Steady persistence in a course of action, a purpose, a state, etc., esp. in spite of difficulties, obstacles, or discouragement.

Definition from dictionary.com

> "Success seems to be connected with action. Successful people keep moving. They make mistakes, but they don't quit."
> ——Conrad Hilton

Victory Dance! – Rewardin

> "The more you praise and cel-ebrate your life, the more there is in life to celebrate."
>
> —Oprah Winfrey

Of course, most hard efforts don't end in failure. Most efforts reap glorious rewards! If you're studying and fine-tuning your test-taking skills and seeing the results, don't forget to celebrate.

As important as pushing yourself is congratulating yourself. When you know how to pat yourself on the back and allow yourself the perks of your success, you're creating your own motivation for keeping up the good work.

A high score on a test and a step close to getting an overall A in a class? Nice. A leisurely afternoon relaxing by the pool after the test is over and done with? Nicer.

PARENT SPEAK

Noticing your child's successes is just as important as trying to help them through their failures. Tell your kids you're proud of them!

Yourself

Life is about balance, so work hard, and play hard. Once you see the fruits of your labor, take the time to enjoy them. It will remind you what all the hard work is for and keep you motivated throughout your life.

The way to learn to do things is to do things. The way to learn a trade is to work at it. Success teaches how to succeed. Begin with the determination to succeed, and the work is half done already.

—Unknown

PARENT SPEAK

It's normal, and admirable, to want to keep your student on track with their schoolwork and activities. But remember that kids burn out, too, so make sure you not only allow them time to celebrate their achievements, but teach them how to fully embrace their successes--and the joys they bring.

Juiced – (Setting Up Your Own Incentive

PARENT SPEAK

Get involved in your child's incentive system. Don't necessarily offer rewards, but help them find their own methods of rewarding themselves that are truly fulfilling. Encourage creativity and reward systems that encourage healthy behaviors. Remember, you're helping to build a life's foundation.

W hen you were a tiny tot, your doctor gave you a lollipop for taking your immunization shots with a stiff upper lip (who are we kidding. You got that lolly even if you bawled your head off, didn't you?). When you were in grade school, your parents might have given you a nice crisp five-dollar bill for every A on your report card.

You may have noticed these types of rewards petering off as you approached your teen years. This is probably because the prevailing school of thought is that as you grow older, you learn that doing the right thing and working hard are their own rewards.

But c'mon. Let's face it. Adults don't always do things for the pure joy of it. More often than not, they're doing their jobs for the paycheck rather than for their sense of duty. So why shouldn't you have incentive for doing well in school?

If no one's offering you incentives, make up your own. Tell yourself that if you get an A on the next test you take, you'll buy that new purse or that

ystem)

videogame you've been eyeing in the mall. Or maybe promise yourself a completely free Saturday, when you won't be touching anything school related if you show major improvement on that big test that's coming up.

Let's get real: you're more likely to study harder if there's a light at the end of the tunnel, even if you have to be the one to shine it. Having an incentive system is a great way to make sure that you're meeting short and long term goals by breaking up the work that needs to be done.

THE BASICS

incentive
n. 1. Something that incites or tends to incite to action or greater effort, as a reward offered for increased productivity.
adj. 2. inciting, as to action; stimulating; provocative

Definition from dictionary.com

"An episode of my favorite comedy is a perfect study break — it's a guaranteed half-hour of laughter that I know won't turn into an entire day of slacking."

Jazzed – (Taking Time to Celebrate)

FOOD FOR THOUGHT

Kids that make time to have fun, separate of school work and guilt free, actually do better in school. So make time for work—and lots of time for play. You'll be glad you did.

Party of one? That's no fun!

Letting others in on your successes makes for a much better celebration, so set yourself up for the sweetest victory possible. As you're studying hard, let your parents in on your process. Let them know you're really giving a test your full attention, and your best shot.

They'll be there to support you, and they'll know just how much you deserve it when you come home with the results you hoped for. When you

Live and work but do not forget to play, to have fun in life and really enjoy it.

—Eileen Caddy

perform to your own expectations, it's reason to be proud. When you perform to your own expectations and exceed everyone else's, it's reason to celebrate.

Get your parents to take you out to a nice restaurant. Or at least get a round of high fives!

Taking the time to pat yourself on the back and bask in your own glory can do a lot to remind you of exactly why you're working so hard.

F.Y.I.

Whether it's something simple like going to dinner or a movie, or maybe something more elaborate like a themed party, having your celebration in mind will be just one more motivation to help you prepare for the big test you'll be celebrating.

"What do we lose by another's good fortune? Let us celebrate with them, or strive to emulate them. That should be our desire and determination."

—Sri Sathya Baba

Amped (Being Proud of Your Gains)

As your test-taking skills improve, it's always helpful to allow yourself a retrospective. Look back on where you started and realize how far you've come. Think about the ways your memory has improved, the ways your comprehension and comfort level have all improved.

Think about the grades you've earned and the ones you've raised.

A constant and small measure of dissatisfaction in yourself is, of course, always to be desired because it pushes you to work harder, to aspire to

FOOD FOR THOUGHT

Getting better at test taking is not an ability, it is a skill that is developed over time.

" To be able to look back upon one's life in satisfaction is to live twice. "

—Kahlil Gibran

greater things. But being able to take stock of your gains and being proud of yourself is key to your long-term happiness and your ability to realistically assess where you started, where you're at, and where you want to be.

Taking time to evaluate how far you've come and how far you have to go is an important part of the process. It's a skill that you'll use not just for test prep in high school, but throughout college, and eventually, your career. A critical part of doing a good job is the ability to look at your own progress objectively and see how you measure up according to your own standards and other people's performances.

THE BASICS

retrospect

n. 1. Contemplation of the past; a survey of past time, events.

v. 2. To look back in thought, refer back.

"Once we believe in ourselves, we can risk curiosity, wonder, spontaneous delight, or any experience that reveals the human spirit."

—e.e. cummings

Pumped – (Not Losing Steam)

As with anything, being proud of your hard-earned test scores and acquired test-prep and test-taking skills should not make you arrogant. Why? Because assuming that you're more awesome than you are leads to laziness, and laziness leads to backsliding.

Make sure the rewards you allow yourself are proportionate to your successes. Acing a pop quiz shouldn't be reason/excuse for you to blow off studying all day for some celebratory video-gaming or shopping.

Keep your goals in sight and don't let yourself give in to indulgences and distractions. After all... you're awesome, but you could always be... awesomer!

FOOD FOR THOUGHT

Remember to acknowledge the progress you make toward your goals. If you set realistic goals, you can achieve them. And while there's no greater reward, reward yourself anyway.

"The journey is the reward."

—Chinese Proverb

As with everything in life, the key to balancing success and hard work is moderation. So work hard, do well, and celebrate those big achievements, but remember that there is always more work to do, and that means you're going have even more to celebrate in the future!

PARENT SPEAK

Sometimes it's the parents' job to balance out the student's perspective on studying – make sure your student recognizes his or her accomplishments and takes time to enjoy them, and also help your child stay on track.

"You are never too old to set another goal or to dream a new dream."

—C. S. Lewis

You Are Ready

> Self-confidence is the first requisite to great undertakings.
>
> —Samuel Johnson

You're probably your biggest critic, but the people around you might sometimes seem to be challenging you for the title. With all the pressure to do well on tests coming from your parents, your teachers, the colleges, and from yourself, you might often feel that you're going to buckle, and that you just can't do as well as everyone wants you to.

Remember that your parents and teachers want you to do well because they care about you and sometimes the pressure you feel from them is

F.Y.I.

Study Skills Tip

Making outlines is a handy way to stay focused on the main points. Outline the most important details of a subject you're studying, and fill in the specifics underneath each of these headings. Outlines are also easy to review with before a test, and a good way to see what you've studied at-a-glance and feel good about it.

just misplaced support. They want you to do well and they know that you can. Now, you just have to show them, and yourself, that with the right preparation and hard work, you can do anything you set your mind to. Don't let self-doubt or any outside criticism get you down and make you feel like you can't do it.

You can. As we said in the beginning, a large part of doing well on tests depends on knowing the tricks of properly preparing, and knowing how to get into test-taking mode. In a way, you just need to find your groove, find what works best for you, and you'll see some vast improvements in your scores.

It's a game you have to master, and even with your occasional self-doubts, know that you are ready.

Pressure makes diamonds.

—General George S. Patton

FOOD FOR THOUGHT

Surround yourself with friends who will encourage you — and whom you can encourage, too! — instead of downers with negative attitudes.

Bring Your A–Game

FOOD FOR THOUGHT

In a 2000 poll conducted by Junior Achievement, Inc., it was found that when asked, "Do you think you will ever have your ideal job," two thirds of teens polled said "definitely" or "pretty sure."

Confidence is key.

Having enough confidence that you're going to do well on a test is largely a result of knowing you've done everything you could to prepare yourself. With your mind filled with newly-acquired knowledge, you can face down a test filled with even the most daunting of questions, because you know you have the right tools and weapons in your arsenal. So step one: be prepared.

"The greatest barrier to success is the fear of failure."

—Sven Goran Eriksson

Being confident on test day allows you to keep your cool so you can focus and concentrate. It also allows you to waste less time second-guessing yourself and agonizing over questions that you've already answered correctly anyway.

Make it a policy to walk into class on test-day as if you own the place. Bring your A-game. Remember that confidence helps you succeed and success makes you confident. Start the cycle!

> Go confidently in the direction of your dreams. Live the life you have imagined.
>
> —Henry David Thoreau

DR. LISA SAYS...

Learning how to study for tests the right way may seem extremely difficult at first, but it won't always be that way. When you really learn the material, you'll have more to build on in the future. You'll start to recognize concepts that repeat or overlap, so you won't have to re-learn them. It also will be easier to memorize new information when you have some basic knowledge to connect it to. You'll also learn the strategies that work best for you, so you can be more efficient with your time. Like anything else that you have had to learn to do, just hang in there, and it will get easier with time!

Remember: Your Best is Good Enough

DR. LISA SAYS...

I still have a card that my parents got me when I was in junior high. It shows a picture of a startled man suddenly realizing that nobody cares what his GPA was. I guess that gives you a sense of what kind of stressed-out teenager I was! I keep the card because it is so simple and true. Since the day I graduated, no one has asked me what my grades were. I rarely tell people where I went to school, because NO ONE CARES. They just care about how well I do my job on a daily basis. That ability comes from the work I put in while I was in school, not from the ranking of the school I went to.

At the end of the day, your best is good enough, even if your teacher seems to disagree. If you can honestly say to yourself that you've done your best, that you've done everything you could to be prepared for a test, then you've done everything right and shouldn't be bothered by the result of a test.

Life is unpredictable. Sometimes a teacher may just not like your style. Sometimes a subject matter is just beyond the reach of your comprehension. Some people are great at math and science, and others are better at English and history; that's just the way we're made!

You don't have to be perfect at everything, but if you've

tried your best, you haven't lost out on any opportunities to learn and grow and practice. And though your best efforts may not be accurately reflected in a test score here or there, the habit of putting forth your best efforts will serve you all your life.

So test your abilities, test your concentration and intelligence, test your endurance. Eventually, it'll all pay off.

F.Y.I.

Ralph Waldo Emerson said, "Insist on yourself; never imitate." Knowing your strengths AND your weaknesses will help you out in the long run — don't overestimate one category and underestimate the other! It's all a part of what makes you you.

" I do the very best I know how, the very best I can, and I mean to keep on doing so until the end. "

—Abraham Lincoln

Fighting Off What's Fightin

What Is It and How Can I Get Rid of It?

I'm so stressed," is something you've probably heard your friends say on almost a daily basis. Recently, you even find yourself chiming in with them when they complain about the mounds of homework they have or all their after school commitments. But what is stress really??

THE BASICS

stress
n. a specific response by the body to a stimu-lus, as fear or pain, that disturbs or interferes with the normal physiological equilibrium of an organism.

physical, mental, or emotional strain or tension: "Worry over his job and his wife's health put him under a great stress."

a situation, occurrence, or factor causing this: "The stress of being trapped in the elevator gave him a pounding headache."

You: Stress Management

Stress is the way your body reacts to demands placed on it, whether that's your upcoming advanced Algebra exam or dealing with a difficult friend. When you feel stressed by something, your body releases chemicals into your bloodstream. These chemicals can have both positive and negative effects. Sometimes stress makes you work harder to get something done, but stress can also slow you down, especially if you have no way to deal with the extra energy the chemicals produce in you.

Here, we'll help you understand the causes of stress, signs of stress, how stress affects you, and the best ways to deal with it, because when you've already got so much to do, stress is the last thing you need to worry about.

FOOD FOR THOUGHT

Many studies suggest that as students get to college, their sleeping schedule suffers greatly. Lack of sleep often results in the inability to concentrate, the need for more naps, and constant fatigue. Try getting a good rest and maybe this will give you more strength to deal with school and other issues.

" For fast-acting relief, try slowing down. "

—Lily Tomlin

Whadda Mean, Take a Deep Breath?

PARENT SPEAK

No one wants to believe that they've overlooked stress overload in their son or daughter. Here are a few signs to look for:

✓ high anxiety, which can lead to panic attacks

✓ feeling pressured, hassled, and hurried all the time

✓ mood swings and irritability

✓ physical symptoms: stomach problems, headaches, chest pain

✓ allergic reaction: eczema or asthma

✓ insomnia

✓ overeating, or worse, smoking or doing drugs

✓ depression

Stress affects everybody differently. Some people express themselves as angry or frustrated when stressed, while others can become withdrawn or depressed. None of these are healthy and each can come with its own set of problems. People who take their aggressions out on people around them tend to alienate friends and loved ones while those who internalize stress can develop unhealthy ways of coping such as eating disorders or substance abuse problems. As if you weren't stressed enough, already...

Believe it or not, stress is not always a bad thing, and it's very normal. It's your body's way of reacting to any change, whether it's positive or negative. And you've probably already figured out that stress is going to be with you throughout your school career—so the sooner you learn how to manage it, the better you'll be.

One of the first things people will tell you to do is 'take a deep breath.' What does that mean, really? Simply put: Stop for a moment. Sometimes you just need to step back and get some perspective on the situation for it to begin making sense. When we're stressed, our minds and bodies have a way of taking over, making it pretty hard to think straight. What can you do to 'take a breath' and get some perspective?

✎ Get up and walk away from the computer or desk.

✎ Go for a short walk (or whatever exercise makes you feel better).

✎ Call a friend and talk about a lot of nothing for a while.

✎ Take a short nap.

✎ Listen to your favorite music.

FOOD FOR THOUGHT

A recent study revealed that over 60% of teenagers say that they watch more than 20 hours of television per week. The main reason? For relaxation.

How Can I Quiet My Mind with All These

FOOD FOR THOUGHT

Students who have learned to manage stress in their daily lives report that the following five items have helped them:

✓ Making a to-do list

✓ Setting realistic goals, both short- and long-term

✓ Stopping the cycle of worrying about "what if?"

✓ Avoiding over-scheduling

✓ Turning mistakes into lessons

When stress tightens its grip on you, it seems like there's no getting away. You may feel anxious, tired, frightened or angry and might not know how to deal with these emotions.

The truth is, everyone feels this way sometimes. It's not about the stress, it's about what you do with it. Sounds silly, right? But it's true.

The best way to deal with stress is not to avoid it, which is impossible, but to learn how to work with it. Here are a few suggestions for thinking about yourself and your well-being first:

✎ Try breathing exercises.

✎ Make an effort to think positively.

✎ Make time to relax and take a break.

✎ Read something uplifting or inspirational.

✎ Use positive visualization techniques—if you see it, you can do it!

✎ Talk it out with a friend or counselor.

oices?

✎ Don't focus on the negative.

✎ Take pride in your accomplishments.

✎ Allow yourself to make some mistakes.

✎ Eat something healthy.

✎ Exercise.

✎ Find something outside of school you like to do, and do it.

✎ Make time for fun!

F.Y.I.

Use these four steps to problem solving:

1. Brainstorm solutions
2. Think of the consequences
3. Choose a solution
4. Evaluate your choice

"Don't under-estimate the value of doing noth-ing, of just going along, listening to all the things you can't hear, and not bothering."
—Pooh's Little Instruction Book, inspired by A.A. Milne

What Is It? Move or Sit Still?

Depending on your personality, different types of exercise may help you relieve stress. Yoga, which emphasizes quiet mediation, a focus on breathing, and lots of stretching and strengthening, can be great therapy for stress management.

FOOD FOR THOUGHT

A half an hour of exercise at least three times a week is an excellent way to get into shape and keep your body less tense. Start by walking around the neighborhood or maybe even enjoying a dance workout video!

"Part of being a winner is knowing when enough is enough. Sometimes you have to give up the fight and walk away, and move on to something that's more productive."

—Donald Trump

Yoga, is a non-competitive activity that gives everyone a chance to move at their own pace and focus on their own personal growth. With a competitive environment at school, yoga can give you the "breathing room" you need to deal with that stress.

Yoga is exercise that is good for the mind, body and soul and is an excellent outlet for those needing a little more quiet time in their lives. Sometimes when life is hectic, the best thing you can do is slow down and take some deep breaths.

F.Y.I.

Does Yoga seem too slow for you? Are you more into fast paced workouts? Try the new "hip" thing: Power Yoga. Power Yoga is essentially yoga with more swift and dynamic movements. It still gives your body that flexibility and ease, but also keeps you awake and refreshed!

" I never thought I had time for exercise until I started going with my roommate. Now I can't imagine not going. "

Exercise Does Calm the Body

FOOD FOR THOUGHT

Exercise is necessary for students because of the related cognitive benefits. What does that mean? When you move your body, your brain works better.
Enough said.

F or those who need to move around to burn off that extra energy, a high paced cardio workout might be a better solution. Something a simple as going for a run or jumping rope can allow you to focus again.

You don't have to go to the gym to get a good workout. You can take a run in your neighborhood or hike in the local park or foothills. When you're short on time, you can take a walk, get some fresh air, and burn a little stress energy.

"There are thousands of causes for stress, and one antidote is to stress is self-expression. That's what happens to me. My thoughts get off my chest."

—Garson Kanin

Like a more structured routine? Sign up for an aerobic or spinning class or try kick boxing. Not only will you work out some aggressions, you'll build up some stamina, too.

Getting into a fitness routine doesn't have to be complicated—it's supposed to take your mind off stress. Enlisting a friend or workout buddy commits you to regular workouts and the time spent with someone you enjoy has added health benefits.

Try scheduling your exercise in with your other appointments. Not only will you be more inclined to show up and get moving, you'll avoid the guilt of missed workouts.

F.Y.I

According to recent studies, more than 70 million Americans walk to work out, making it the most popular form of exercise.

I'm really into my running workout. Running really helps me clear my head and makes me feel good, especially when I'm stressed.

—Katie Holmes

RESOURCES

Below are some great web resources for you and your parents to check out:

www.4Parents.org

www.AboveTheInfluence.com

www.TheCoolSpot.gov

www.DrDrew.com

www.Education.com

www.GirlsSpeakOut.org

www.IWannaKnow.org

www.Kaplan.com

www.KidsHealth.org

www.ParentingTeens.About.com

www.PreteenAlliance.org

www.ReachOut.com.au

www.TeenAdvice.About.com

THINGS TO THINK ABOUT

We've left you room to jot down notes of issues you want to discuss
with friends, teachers or parents. We hope you use these pages as you read
to personalize this book, and make it your own.

THINGS TO TALK TO MY
TEACHERS/PARENTS ABOUT

THINGS TO TALK TO MY FRIENDS ABOUT

Want more help dealing with the stress in your life? Look for these other books from Kaplan Publishing. Available wherever books are sold:

SOS Guide to Handling Peer Pressure
(Available in September 2008)

SOS Guide to Saying No to Cheating
(Available in September 2008)

SOS Guide to Managing Your Time
(Available in March 2009)

SOS Guide to Getting Into Clubs and Sports
(Available in March 2009)

SOS Guide to Tackling Your Homework
(Available in March 2009)

Do your parents need a refresher course when it comes time to help you or your siblings with math homework? Tell them about:

Kaplan's Math for Moms and Dads
(Available October 2008)
This primer gives them all the terms, concepts, and helpful tips they've forgotten since high school.